Past Chains

By

Esha Montgomery

Copyright Print

Dedication

I would like to dedicate this book to my awesome family, the people I see in passing, fellow poets and my partner without whom my quest to pursue poetry and love would be frivolous. Thank you for your kind words and continued support. This is for all those who are in search of peace in the storm. Keep fighting the good fight. Last but not least, I would like to thank God for making me whole again.

Sincerely, Esha

Table of Contents

Introduction

We all deserve our own little slice of happiness. A reason to break free from past chains and see value in ourselves. A reason to feel hopeful and optimistic in a time of fear and doubt. A reason to keep pushing back against systematic oppression in the face of financial uncertainty. A reason to love and trust again. A reason to expect a silver lining beneath the storm. This chapbook is that reason for me. I wrote it with the intent of sharing my sunny disposition with you. I pray this book grants peace and healing to all that read it.

Part 1

Boxer

you do it for me every time,
melanated children of God
with skin like shining bronze,
your hair stands proud and tall
like freshly baked muffins
rising under a moonlit sky,

your teeth like rows of handpicked pearls
coated in glory,
even when one goes missing
you are the darling of excellence
and the kitchen beautician,

the bringer of peace
and war's ammunition,
cream of the crop
and servant of the field
i see you in everything

creator of cool,
the inventor of bling,
they force you into concrete cells
with reinforced steel bars
to drudge in their prison mills
for $15.00 a day

your children miss you
they ask their mother,
why you've gone away

but she say, you'll be back soon
lies told to young responsive ears
ready to receive good news

but i see you,
descendent of slaves and kings
rolled all into one
your people labored
underneath the hot, southern, plantation sun

robbed of your African identity
and denied monies owed
paying the price
of being the oppressed,
whose identity is bought and sold

but your children are breaking free
like seashells taken to the deep
by the tide's wave
your people sparked the American Revolution
when Crispus Attucks died brave

you built a country
that you have never been equipped to call home
stolen from your family
and all you own
the salt of your tears
marked by blood and bone

still, i see you
as your community

is lulled to silence
by siren cries
and officer that points
the gun at you
does so with lifeless eyes

but you prevail
like a mighty oak tree
digging your roots ever deeper
so that your traditions will carve a path
for your people
in a frightfully chilled world

snuggled in my heart's bedrock
i can feel the dominion of my mother's arms
as she rocked me to sleep
singing songs of orange day break
and black jubilee

a life more abundant
calls for you and me
no matter how hard,
the wind may blow:
hail, fog or tornado
you make me believe

we are a divine people
forged from Saturn's ring
the residue of Malcolm's struggle
and the hope of Martian's dreams
we are anger and love

birthed from stardust and moonbeams

we are the boxer
that practiced for centuries
waging an enduring match
with solace in our aching brows
and sweat on our broad backs
yet we keep on fighting
and you do it for me every time…

Paper Mache

heart wrapped in paper mache
coming undone
as fields of poppy seeds
send my mind my into overdrive

do drugs make me feel alive?
or is it all a lie?
cover up the tears falling inside
like rivers of tribune
that never run dry

how do i...
break the rat race
one check away from abandoned lots
6 figures away from sizeable income
what you do to fill the hole
may not buy you freedom

let's reconcile -if you're sorry
i'm sorry too
bear hug and let go!!!
bridge the gulf in the equality gap
and make two halves whole

but the rich don't want that though
they scared of the elements
what it's like with no shelter, 50 below
they want the sunshine glow

the ice that don't drip
but the wrist is froze
unless we talking Aspen style
they hate the snow!

and people who tasted the bottom
shake at the thought of money getting low
so they turn their back on the people
and the communities they use to know

let's stop fighting over parties
let's fight to save the youth
no more closed door politics
tell families struggling to survive the truth

how do i...
break the rat race
one check away from abandoned lots
6 figures away from sizeable income
what you do to fill the hole
may not buy you freedom

something deeper than me versus you
if you collect my tax dollars
where is the wealth going to
feeding the 1%
at the cost of my chipped tooth

poor people are left to pay the debt
the rich circumvented
so when i'm ready to retire

there will be no pension

did i fail to mention
college costs are over inflated
loan enhanced debt covers college tuition
rage hits a fork road
when determination succumbs
to job ambitions
you want to do more
but Sallie Mae payments call for retention

we push and pull
for nights and days
at a situation that stays the same

the poor carries the load
and takes the blame
the middle class kill their time
to keep some skin in the game

one check away from abandoned lots
6 figures away from sizeable income
what you do to fill the hole
may not buy you freedom

to uphold the status quo
we blindfold the stress we see
invisible are those in need
they beg for change
but we don't have the emotional means

to raise above requires greed
stiff upper lip and act mean
the things we do
to maintain the machine
so i wrapped my heart in paper mache

Call of the Wild

ripples send repetitive lines down a reflection
brilliant shield of mine
take what is not art and leave
but in the midst of your bloodletting
don't forget about me

fangs that once sunk fear
into soft and giving skin
cannot prick angry kevlar intent
i use to feed my ambitions with your lies
now you can't buy time

little black book tucked
into social media pages
i told you about that shit

my scorn will beat you
with the switch
your grandma whipped your mother with
the things you do cheapen you

slice through hurt's glass
make a robbed and tortured soul laugh
like you use to
before i knew
what you were up to

before admiration
flipped to fuck you

back when
i wanted to cuff you

you care selfishly
never wondering about what we needed
only thinking about what you need
you had a glimpse
but will never take in the breath of me

black sores ripped open
back tracking on past wounds
with new glaze, chewing tobacco and antiseptic
old tricks still not working

green pus leaking from an abscess
you could of left alone
too busy poking at sour romance scabs,
i thought were healed,
instead of focusing on home

marks on my heart
point to where the pain is
truth evades your lips
so you chop it up as blameless

slice through hurt's glass
make a robbed and tortured soul laugh
like you use to
before i knew
what you were up to

before admiration
flipped to fuck you
back when
i wanted to cuff you

turquoise shades of grey
create diagonal lines across pertinacious streets
the smile of new men beckon me
from the comfort of factious tranquility
a life created to silence me
only to find myself imbedded in backcountry roads
a return to lone wolf mentality

Daddy

*You always complain about how I don't show I love
you enough. I hope this poem does you justice*

before speech was attributed to words
before freshly created ears heard
before feet met broken pavement
in a cohesive strut

you called me your baby girl
and picked me up
as my youth brought on the coming spring
you took me fishing

the riverbank was my backyard
and we took to the land
when times were hard

i remember when momma used to say
you wanna go see Daddy?
i would nod my head in glee
Mom would strap me up in the car seat

you were always
just a few yards away in my mind
never gone too long
never hard to find

before speech was attributed to words
before freshly created ears heard

before feet met broken pavement
in a cohesive strut

back when i was confounded
by the complexities of riding a bike
we tried for hours
but couldn't get past 2 blocks

most people... would of told me give up
but you said don't stop
20 years later
i am proud to say,
i can ride about... a good 4 blocks

before i went through
my girlhood transformation and wrestled
with the birds and bees initiation
before you allowed lipstick on my lips
before boys made their way to uncharted hips
you were a friend to me

a 6 ft Hercules
that would do whatever necessary to protect
my mother and me
and i adore you for it
some men might walk away from their responsibilities
but you never ignored it

He Bellows

from the rhythmic feel of his fingers tapping
to the aesthetic look of his fro
he's one of the best musicians out
but the world will never know

his clothes second hand
but he's clean though
from the stone washed, ripped denim jeans
to his weather worn shoes

bicycling his stress away
avoiding the creation of CO_2
he sleeps well at night

some say he is too careful
about the things he consumes
but if fast food is empty calories,
why leave room?

he is, the guitar player
in the L train station
unaware of time
he got a lot to say
but much more on his mind

he sings to the tune of climate change
and you throw dimes
his baritone is sea deep
as he bellows:

gonna liberate you
wait and see
the real danger your running from
gonna make you thirsty

Antarctica is melting
do we care?
his eyes met, blank looks
and puzzled stares

what are we gonna leave?
the next generation deserves more
than smart phones and flat screen TVs
what are they gonna eat?

trophy hunters take it for granted
life thriving as nature planned it
they strike fear into deer at play
bear cubs learn to stay away

danger afoot in the woods,
these days…
watch them as they watch you
looking for tracts of something new
wall space is bare
looking for an animal's head to give it too

i'm gonna liberate you
wait and see
the real danger your running from

gonna make you thirsty

he ends his set
a couple dollars ahead,
packs up his belongings
and heads home
every time he performs for strangers
he feels a little less alone

he is, the guitar player
in the L train station
unaware of time
he got a lot to say
but much more on his mind

Gym Body

are we spoiled acting?
pleading for a better life
but too afraid to take action
i take to fasting

i been drinking so poorly
my blood taste like fruit passion
the gym worries me
ya know?
the sit-ups, I don't feel inclined to do

because my stomach ain't tight
and i was eating pork chops last night
seems like the new year resolution
was the easy part
how do i get past start?

and oh Lord the sweat
shimming down my temples
it's like sitting under a mid-July sun
with a slight overcast

that's a bit of relief
but it don't last
and why the treadmill feel like
it's going too fast
i gotta hit stop
before i fall off
and bust my ass

no, no, no…
let me talk about it
the workout keep hitting me back
i get going good, then the next day
my muscles are out of whack

they feel tight and strained
my back popping like popcorn
in the microwave
and the damn limp
that rested in my right leg
people laughing at me
cuz i'm moving like i got a peg

that's what I get
for going to the gym the other night
now I gotta wobble
cause my high not acting right

Ode to My Mother

the rusted out lemon with the backdoor
that couldn't close all the way,
parked outside your
Southern, widowed, mother's driveway
couldn't get you to your destination on time

carved from travel brochures
of a land outside of time
shining castle on a hill in the summertime
you made a mac, hustler and ex-player
dressed in silk from head to toe
from the burbs, above Chicago,
love you

first date was lively:
pink cotton candy spun by cupid's bow,
wet rides that made you wet
corn dogs, giant drops
and amusement park thrill
you will never forget

wholesome tales your children were later, satisfied
with
but your Mom cared nothing for your romantic
endeavor
saw you fixing to move on
and didn't want change

what did ya Mother do?

ignored the seeds birthed by you
had a… my way or the highway attitude
Grandma was missing in action
gone from the family life
her daughter was inspired to start
no love lost, no love gained

a first time mother with no motherly support
but who did she really hurt
her selfish, dignified lies
spread to bread like hazel Nutella on rye
too busy to babysit, smeared on her lips

behide the red rope
to the catholic charities stronghold
was a naive young wife,
let down by systemic racism
she did not earn but was forced to endure

i watched translucent faith covered spheres
fall from my mother's slanted eyes
i caught salty tears with my 3 year old finger tips
And said, *Mommy please don't cry*
26 years later,
i am still here
to dry her eyes

Brewing Coffee

it was the 90's feel
charging the apartment
with the tunes of Sade
damn,
i use to love the rhythm
that possessed my feet
whenever,
smooth operator played

hi guys, we gotta straighten out this living room
6am and my Dad
is at it again
with the vacuum
it's the early 2000's
and XM Sirius radio
replaced household tunes

my Mom is stirred
by the sound
she overheard
breakfast will be ready soon
The sun rose
with the smell of coffee she brewed

It's 2010,
we a decade in
to what I don't know
but my mother lost her ability
to cry years ago

Dad is different now
4 layoffs
And no pension to show
far removed from the man
i loved and knew
we are strangers awaiting familial doom

he's given up on improvement
and his family's future too
The relationship was a casualty
of the hopes and dreams
that poverty consumes
Still the sun rose
with the smell of coffee he brewed

7 years in
and things getting worse
this sickness is my blessing
and my curse
the very thing that crippled my father
made me my mother's nurse

malnutritioned dreams
fed on IV's
took away my father's… *Why?*
the nights once filled with laughter
were drowned out
by ESPN's might

be mad! stomp! shout!

the working man died
when the factories moved out
but instead your sadness grew
what can a black man
without an education do?
but the sun rose with the smell of coffee he brewed

Part 2

Giving Hands

giving hands
turn ruby red
like Moroccan clay
people you helped in the past
won't talk to you today
what am i gonna do with you?
pray

belly swollen
and empty
here's to looking full
eyes bright and clear as day
till they pull the wool

lean in
to listen
and say, *awe*
but won't aid
yo living condition at all

watched yo demise
applauding for encore
at your fall
but stunt when you come round
talkin bout, *stand tall*

giving hands
turn ruby red
like Moroccan clay

people you helped in the past
won't talk to you today
what am i gonna do for you?
pray

lights cut out
Comed ain't cheap
bills is steep
pockets anything but deep
but as the rich hold gabfest
the poor get no sleep
children to feed
2 jobs
and a side hustle before sleep

but did you hear me
turn up the loud speaker
in a quiet house
if you feel me
the rich get richer
and the poor get along nearly

lies can make
a clean house filthy
people mean well
with a lifestyle that's guilty

they need you
in every way down but up
the deterioration of your relation
only seemed abrupt

so when they blowing
down your line
cuz you doing better
you know what's up

giving hands
turn ruby red
like Moroccan clay
people you helped in the past
won't talk to you today
what am i gonna do for you?
pray

Graffiti Outside

graffiti outside the station's walls
looks like poetry in motion to me
people waiting to add something more
than piss and moonshine to concrete

i get a whiff of it
every time i venture on a commute
people hear the cries
but earphones makes their sadness mute

it's the smell of corporate corruption
the sting of indifference
towards homelessness, poverty and disabled folk
there are enough resources to go around
but the system's broke

an ever present alarm going off
but no one at home is woke
we shift like thighs from side to side
when passion makes us quake
but the moment of climax feelings dissipate

graffiti outside the station's walls
looks like poetry in motion to me
people waiting to add something more
than piss and moonshine to concrete

Guilt Personified

fields of roses open wide for you
April showers have awaken me
baby dolls with no pacifier
i'm sorry jelly bean
sorry my becoming a mother too soon
spelled doom for your waiting room

you had a right
to something greater
than a toilet flush
On to the next
concern of the day
despite my inconsistencies as your barrier
you are the very twinkle of life itself

but deep down
i wanted more for you
than a struggling two parent home
i had no plans
on nursing you with college loans
shallow as it may seem
i put away childhood fantasies
for logic based dreams

my failure as an adult
is not a negative reflection on you
you implanted in my soul
and not just my womb
and did what God called you to do

i wanna acknowledge
that my well intentioned apology
won't cut it

i pushed you out the picture
to make space for me
covering up your existence
due to my iniquity
i'm a killer without a knife

i pulled the trigger
without a gun
you are innocent
and brought harm to no one
your passing won't be in vain
i don't know why I think about you
when it rains

what is a women's role?
to be a breeder, caretaker, or hooded grim reaper
standing outside the gate like a crypt keeper
imagine me with a scythe
i'm the reason you can't sleep at night

to deny my needs
when temptation drives my body to fever
chasing for medicine like a reliever
i'm a primadonna
the giver of life
cradled civilization between the gap in my thighs
i am everyone's momma

i am the baddest bitch
without a lease
vengeance and love reincarnated
in the eyes of your baby niece
i am woman's wrath
yet to be released

when God made Adam
he beckoned for a sister like me
i made his love jones for me
with the rise of my chest

the sun, moon and stars
fall into harmony
i am imperfect perfection
so tell your expectations
i'm sorry

I Apologize to Me the Phoenix

This piece was a writing exercise I created at the writing workshop hosted by Surviving the Mic.

i apologize to me
for every time
i allowed myself to feel down
so that another person
could step up victoriously
only to witness the hostilely
the world has against someone
unwilling to fight for themselves unapologetically

as i look at my present
with grave eyes
unable to see the optimism that lives in me
i am beaten down by the reality
that i am and always have been
my own worst enemy
that is probably the opposite
of what the person standing over me thought
as they unconsciously gave rise
 to the careless side of me

i apologize to me
for every time
i allowed myself to blindly follow
another person's directive
without faith in my own
leaving home ready to believe any stranger,

selling me a false line

just so that i can ignore
a bitter and relentless reality for just a while longer
i *can fake strong*
as the rope I use to hang my ambitions on gets longer
and longer

meanwhile…
i apologize to me
for every time
i allowed myself to live in emotional instability
just because i don't want to say goodbye
to a man that is eating away at me
tearing at the very soul he once swore to protect

instead of packing my bags
i awaited his calls
and silently accepted texts
as though a man who doesn't love himself
knows what's best

even after his mother told me not to accept less
i stand here at his door again
but i turn away
when i see a slither of light creep in
as he opens the door
and i remember that

i apologize to me
for every time

i allowed my dreams to be pummeled
and kicked around
for the sake of appeasing others
while settling for a 24 hour pity party
thrown by the insufferable me
tending to old and new wounds
that won't bleed
staked with pain and misery
because i felt that succumbing
was easier than overcoming
the words of those who mean me ill
but yet and still

i apologize to me
for every time
i allowed the essence of life
to fall from my eyes
instead of pushing forward
like a Ford F-150 truck
on a strenuous mountain drive
i am the fisher man's catch

the aurora borealis without a complex
i am the tendon
that took out your right leg after 8 miles
because you forgot to stretch
i am the tiredness in your yawh
encouraging you to rest
i am the still voice that wonders
what's next

i am the sexiness that breathes life
into the little black dress
i am the power in the black woman
that got all of society feeling pressed

yes, i am as close to wrath
and heaven as it gets
because every time
i allowed myself to burn
i came out a phoenix
so i apologize to me

Ole Shoes

sole done been worn out
from beating feet on Chicago concrete
walk is serious
but the tingle in my feet is discrete

i'm running down on old fantasies
like they owe me refuge
from drive poorly used

these is working man's shoes
they carry the aches
that gave my Dad's dogs the blues

holy dreams birthed by
walking a day in my Mother's heels
i never understood her journey
but maybe someday i will

my sista is a Nike and Jordan chick
more into flats myself
she has a collection a mile long
so if i'm in need
i know where i'm gettin em from

snatch a pair
then prepare to run
my job as a big sis
is never done

sole done been worn out
from beating feet on Chicago concrete
walk is serious
but the tingle in my callus is discrete

Feel Better Soon

he say, he ready now
his head's on steady now
he lost me
and he don't know how
but i do
he made promises
he would never see through

his vision was clouded
the feelings said, stay
but his shallow pockets
wouldn't allow it

when you were tripping
i fell through
covered you in my love and held you

but when my chips were down
and no one was around
you never came through

if your ambition matched your mission
you would have held me too
and comforted me the way lovers do

but you didn't let it show
the next person would never know
that your brokenness, broke you

when you were tripping
i fell through
covered you in my love and held you

so when you call my phone
at 2:30 in the morn
talkin' bout, *i miss you and what's new?*

just know, i'm not alone
and if i were,
i wouldn't invite you back into my home
because i deserve better

whenever i was in need
you'd get fly like feathers
you weren't the type of man to stop through
and make me feel better

Lover's Eve

i get off work at five
he commutes to me
when my shift is done
he is sacred to me
i share his forbidden fruit with no one

we join hands
when heading for the street
he plays in my hair
falls in my eyes
dances in my sea
and makes my ability to resist go weak
the locking of our tongues
does it for me

he makes my 29 feel lovely
but this outward expression of care
makes my world complete
Vodka on my breath
a little black dress and countless successes
couldn't even bring these moments

we join hands
when heading for the street
he plays in my hair
falls in my eyes
dances in my sea

emerald green and crimson red lights

strung on houses, bungalows and duplexes galore
sugar plums, mistletoe, pine cones and anvils
pirouette
over our heads in Christmas Eve delight
santa won't be the only one scaling chimneys tonight

When Love Comes

my love
is always waiting on me
it is patient
and breeds tranquility

my love is daring
and fights for peace
he cares nothing for my past
because he knows
the struggle fostered me

my love is freedom
awakened by a baby's laugh
and wants to have them with me

my love is silence
arriving the morning after the storm
when he's leaving for work
but promising not to be gone too long

my love is a resounding wave
in a calm sea
but the energy i throw at him
can me returned to me
because we are two peas

i ponder about how he came to be
my love is black and bode
and worships me
but can turn green with envy

my love
is always waiting on me

it is patient
and breeds tranquility

my love is thousands of secrets untold
but his eyes speak to my soul
and there you have it
my love is forever young
and never gets old

Till Next Time...

This chapbook means the world to me and I hope you enjoyed it. There were days when I wanted to write but ended up with a blank page staring back at me but eventually the words came. Don't lose faith in your dreams you have all you need to prevail and break free from past chains. Thank you for reading.

Yours Sincerely,

Esha

<u>Notes</u>